CW00607005

MAGICAL MEMORIES

Edited by

Heather Killingray

First published in Great Britain in 2000 by
POETRY NOW
Remus House,
Coltsfoot Drive,
Peterborough, PE2 9JX
Telephone (01733) 898101
Fax (01733) 313524

HB ISBN 0 75432 483 4
SB ISBN 0 75432 484 2

FOREWORD

Although we are a nation of poets we are accused of not reading poetry, or buying poetry books. After many years of listening to the incessant gripes of poetry publishers, I can only assume that the books they publish, in general, are books that most people do not want to read.

Poetry should not be obscure, introverted, and as cryptic as a crossword puzzle: it is the poet's duty to reach out and embrace the world.

The world owes the poet nothing and we should not be expected to dig and delve into a rambling discourse searching for some inner meaning.

The reason we write poetry (and almost all of us do) is because we want to communicate: an ideal; an idea; or a specific feeling.

Poetry is as essential in communication, as a letter; a radio; a telephone, and the main criterion for selecting the poems in this anthology is very simple: they communicate.

CONTENTS

CHILDREN'S JOY

Little ones are such great fun,
In their own way they tell you what must be done.
Not cheekily but with untold grace,
So you have the feeling that jam is being smeared over your face.

Kiddies can hurt unintentionally,
But really they only want to spread plenty of glee.
They look to us to guide them through thick and thin,
And don't really wish to be remembered for any sin.

Sometimes their little faces can be full of trouble,
But an elder can always disperse a nasty bubble.
Then they will be rewarded with a radiant smile,
And the youngsters are full of fun after a while.

As they grow up there are fewer tears,
For they learn to allay so many fears.
They will shoot up fast and wish to be of use,
Bear with them or some of your happiest hours you will lose.

Betty Green

YOUTH

What is this thing called 'Youth'?
It's but a stepping stone on the way of life,
A time when yesterday's carefree children
Are suddenly bewildered in a world of strife.
A time when the right age is uncertain.
When they're much too old for childish toys
And yet, they're told in no uncertain terms
They're still too young for dating girls and boys!
A time when loving, caring parents will insist
Their own moral codes are carried to the letter.
Confusion reigns 'You're much too young for that!'
Or worse still, 'You're old enough to know better!'
It's a time of frustration, temptation and indecision.
When in their many varied ways they ask
For a listening ear, an encouraging word, a helping hand.
For us - 'yesterday's youths' - this is a worthwhile task.
Today's youths are the leaders of tomorrow's world.
Let's show them the way to the next stepping stone.
Give them the caring guidance they deserve.
No one should make the journey all alone.
Now is the time to remember our young people.
In God's world He has a place for each and everyone.
Our task is to show by our good example
The way that life's journey should be run.

Pat Heppel

MY DAUGHTER

I saw her born, adored that child, so beautiful to me,
A precious jewel, a gift so pure, for all the world to see.

I watched her grow, I heard her speak, I saw her first few steps,
At night I'd gaze, in wonderment, as to her cot I crept.

The years passed by, she grew so tall, a beauty to behold,
She laughed and played, she sang and danced, I saw it all unfold.

Her teenage years bought mysteries, emotions yet unknown,
My little girl, my precious child, had to a woman grown.

Sometimes she'd sit upon my knee and say, 'Don't worry Dad,'
Then plant a kiss upon my cheek and make my heart so glad.

She blossomed out and love came in, she met herself a man,
To care for her and make her life complete, as best he can.

She took my arm, walked up the aisle, I felt so full of pride,
She is no more my little girl; I'm father of the Bride.

Jim Sargant

SCHOOL DAYS

At four you get to go to school
But your uniform never fits.
You eat semolina and you learn your sums
And your head gets full of nits.

You go to school on a little red bus
And it leaves at half past eight.
You play in the playground and when the bell rings
You line up at the gate.

If you are good you get to play
With the sand pit by the door.
But if you are naughty the teacher says
'Sit quietly on the floor.'

When you get to seven they make you move
To the junior school next door.
You have to do a lot more sums
And it's not as much fun any more.

But when you get to the top of the school
You can boss everyone about.
You get a nice bright shiny badge,
You're a prefect with some clout.

At the age of eleven you move again
This time to the local High.
You get a blazer and a school badge,
Long trousers and a tie.

The years are weird in High school
You should have exams in your head.
But you start to get whiskers and acne
And you think of girls in bed.

If you're lucky you pass all your exams
And then you get to leave home.
You go on to university
But now that's another poem!

Angela Martinelli

THE AUTISTIC CHILD

He is so very beautiful
An angel, without wings -
He loves all flowers, and water
And shiny tinkling things.

See him on the Norfolk beach
Running to the sea,
Loving life, blue skies and sun,
Happy to be free!

How I long to hold him close
Dear little child aged two,
You are so young and perfect
As you toddle into view.

You do not say you love me -
You never seem to care!
My cherub with the blue eyes
And curly flaxen hair.

You scream with such frustration
And this is just one sign
That you were born autistic
Sad silent child of mine.

Peggy Briston

TINY THOUGHTS

As evening draws nigh and the sunset glows red
I watched my small child slowly climb up to bed.
In pretty pink night-gown, long flowing gold hair
She laughed as she conquered each beckoning stair.

On reaching her bedroom she crept through the door,
Went down on her knees on the bare wooden floor.
Tiny hands clasp together, slowly bowing her head
Said her own little prayer as she knelt by her bed.

Please God, just listen, I've something to say.
Thank you for sending this nice sunny day.
Thanks for my dollies and all other toys.
Thank you for loving all little girls and boys.
Thank you for helping Daddy choose his pretty wife
And bless Mammy for her pains to give me this life.

She looked at me shyly with a cute little grin
Then climbed into bed and pulled the sheet to her chin.
She raised her head slightly to bid me goodnight
Then slipped into her dreams as I turned out the light.

From all the confusion in her tiny sweet head
Was her own special meaning in each word she said.
Lord let her sleep safely in her bed tonight
To spread out her joy in the new morning light.

B Wardle

HERITAGE OF THE LORD 'CHILDREN'

Child so helpless
More precious than gold
Gift from God
To be washed, fed and clothed.
Little eyes, little feet
Pleading eyes for that special treat
Sometimes laughter, sometimes tears
Winning ways not knowing fears.
Responsibility to parents, mould child
As he grows, future destiny God alone knows.
Gracious and loving
Parents need to be strong
Child is your off spring, with pride you may see
Someone climbing high in society.
Yet again, although parents implore
May witness ability pushed
Out the door.
Prayer is the answer never give in
Someday, sometime that soul
You may win.

Children are a heritage of the Lord
Prodigal son returned
To warm welcome
From a waiting father.
Don't give up on your children
Keep a beacon burning some day
You may see your wayward child returning.

Frances Gibson

PURE JOY

The miracle of birth to me
Is a wondrous mystery,
That new born babe - a part of you,
This precious gift of life so new:
'Tis only then you come to know
The love and care you need to show,
From then on it is your quest
To be a parent of the best,
You only get one chance, it's true
To guide them all their childhood through.
You aim to teach as you were taught
For through your childhood you were brought
By your parents, oh so wise,
To adulthood, it's no surprise
That through them you've learned so much,
Above all else that loving touch:
Like them you'll be both firm and fair,
Be young with them, their problems share,
Let them know what's wrong and right
Be there for them both day and night.
Also you'll find your common sense
Will surely come to your defence.
But the thing you most, must prove
To them is never ending love.
Parenting's an awesome task;
The questions kids are apt to ask,
Your patience they may sorely try,
That they're adored you can't deny:
Like as not to them you'll shine,
Your family will turn out fine
And when at last they fly the nest
Your prayer is that you've passed the test.

Peter Fordham

DEAR DAUGHTER

How well I remember the day I first saw you,
That October day, the day that I bore you.
So tiny you were, so soft, so sweet.
From the top of your head, to your small pink feet.
So perfect, so precious, and thank God complete.

I couldn't believe this blessing, this joy,
I now had a girl, as well as a boy.
So we named you Helen, shining light.
This little bundle, who came in the night.
God's greatest gift, and dear to my sight.

Amelia Wilson

DIVIDED WORLDS

We met in college
our happiest days,
a future was planned
as we held hands,
our homes were near
families we loved 'dear',
so end of term
our families met.
But no help, did we get,
far too young,
They made that 'clear'.
We had to part, it broke our hearts
to go our separate ways.
On journeys so unsure
time passes quickly.
As months turned to years
and I never forgot
The girl I loved dear.
So back to the village
I left, long ago,
But time does not stand still
and in the church, on the hill
I saw you there, knelt in prayer.
Knowing now the path you chose.
In the 'steps' of the divine.
now you never, can be mine.

Margaret Parnell

UNWRITTEN LOG

Everything's ready - the day's finally arrived
      New books - new look
In uncharted water, new horizons lie ahead
You are the skipper, to chart your own course
Time comes to leave behind your first mate
      Near to the harbour.
I mustn't be late, but I know he'll wait
Hard work and preparation is now complete
Time has come to stand on your own feet
New friends to make - old hearts to break
Treasurer - painter - writer - who knows
Creative thoughts, are free to flow
You know all the rules and how to behave
Big steps indeed, when you are only five.

David Charles

BABIES - NO THANKS

Having children is not all fun and joy.
Especially if you've got a whinging boy.
Plus there's getting up at three
So they can be sick upon your knee.
Winding, changing nappies is a bore,
Then wide awake again at four.
When they're teething, there's no sleep.
Little babies you can keep.

Don Goodwin

CHILDHOOD

The joys of children touch the heart
An age to which we were a part.
With wondering eyes open wide
We'd not learnt to run or hide.
The candour of pure nakedness
Had no ideologies to redress.

Untarnished by worldly care
Children are so willing to share.
Enthusiasm just at ease
Knows no impartialites.
The simple pleasures of make-believe
Have so many fantasies to retrieve.

But childish images fade away
When other games come to play;
And love once freely given to all
Starts to build its safety wall.
Then 'Never Never Land' just disappears
With the innocence of childhood years.

H D Hensman

JOY OF CHILDREN

It's a joy with children
as you watch them play and laugh.

As you've brought them up
from small to big
and learnt them every step in life.

You've seen them grow
from baby to toddler
to teenager to adult
and seen the change in their lives.

And it won't be long
for them to get married
and have a family.

And it will be a joy for them
as they will watch
their children play and laugh.

Shirin Esat

FOR SISTER, RESIST

Well armed spirit with a sword of faith
And clarion call zeal of Jericho's fall
But Moderator speaks, feels like a waif,
Too wordy the scientific sermon
For world that is a sub-strata of Hell
Seems terse God steering through cloudy
Sky over tidal pull to a safe wharf.

Yet look to starboard the feat to be alert
For what seemed like vocation's fate cut short
Is deference to God whose ways are so strange!

A different dream and desire: dialect
Starting with 'Daddy' - 'Daughter' in effect
New perspective and life for a cradle.
Small Christian 'Sister' to look forward
To your ambition's citadel,
Your family's reward!

Suzanne Stratful

THE TREE OF LIFE!

A new branch in life!
A new baby born,
Way up on a treetop
Whilst floods raged below.

The family home gone
But sweet baby don't cry -
Your mummy protects you
And God is nearby.

Be brave little lady
So Moses was found -
Deep in the Bulrushes
Much water surround.

And he too found haven -
Became a great name,
His faith never faltered
And you'll be the same.

So hush little lady
Sweet destiny calls -
Your future is fame
Your portrait grace halls,

Your purpose? - *Life-giving!*
Its symbol? - *The tree!*
So rest my sweet darling
And stay close with me.

Mary Skelton

BORROWED BABES

Grandchildren have not
been meted out to us;
age is purplish black
and the shadows deepen;
a sunbeam dallies
and the outdoors beckons.
Laughter shudders in
between the crying trees,
dappling sprigs of dream.
Jointly we discover
children by the ponds;
wands weld them to the geese;
squawks of laughter blend,
coalesce with the shrieks
of fluttering bird.
Tiny hands spin crumbs;
water and breeze proffer
a nursery frieze
and startlingly pink wheel
on ways between leaves,
reveal a darling's toes.
She's someone else's.
Together we look on;
ducks and dear infants
pluck at the years we lose,
divest us of 'the blues'
by grey and silver pond life
whilst, light-hearted, we partake
of youth,
nostalgic over yesterdays.

Ruth Daviat

THE BABY GIRL

The baby girl kicked in her cradle.
Her laughter with joy filled the air.
She loved life in all its profusion.
Her days held no sorrow or care.

As she shook her rattle with gusto
The cradle swung gently in time.
It swayed to and fro on its rockers
As though it were acting a mime.

Her golden hair spread on the pillow
Her blue eyes wide open to view
The world hurrying on its business
She lay there quite happy to coo.

Her bright and inquisitive glances
Took in all the sights of the room:
The table, the chairs and the sideboard,
The sofa, the dustpan, the broom.

As Mother went past her she giggled,
Help up little arms hopefully.
She clutched Mother's thumb with her fingers
She loved her, 'twas easy to see.

My little one, may you be happy.
May life treat you well all your days
And faith, hope and love be your portion,
Good fortune be with you always.

Joyce M Turner

A DREAM COME TRUE

All our dreams had just come true
There you lay all dressed in blue,
As our lives made room for you
Day by day you grew and grew,
Then off to play-group you were sent
Hours you played there happily spent,
Then came primary school, first day,
You really began to grow away.

Secondary school came so fast
How quickly all the years went past,
In no time at all, those terrible teens
All designer shirts and denim jeans,
The day you brought that first girl home
A day we all began to moan,
Our son's grown up so fast
Eighteen years have just gone past,
That first offer to pay your way
Home from work on your first pay day.

Although you are a child no more
Of this you can be very sure,
In good times or bad, happy or sad
You can always rely on your mum and dad.

S Walters

MY NIECES

Gold,
Diamonds,
Rubies and pearls,
Are nothing when placed next to my girls.
For their eyes shine brighter than diamonds,
Their hair is prettier than gold,
Their lips are redder than rubies,
And what may you ask of the pearls,
They're just raindrops compared to my girls.

M Murphy

WEDDING DAY

Through the slits of greyness,
I see the misty, floating dress,
Waiting like mine so long ago
For the bride and her new life.

We rise, jostling for the shower,
When pristine we drink our rescue
Flower remedies and nibble little,
Rushing to hair care and titivating -
More tea is brewed, our calming balm,
Bouquets arrive and buttonholes,
Wafts of lilies, perfume sprays,
Silken legs slide on petticoats.

Ready at last I leave for church,
Hugging and air-kissing, my loves
Left to be driven together -
My hyacinth crown, queen bee hat
Is lifting and bridesmaids giggle,
Hitching their wild silk hems as we go.
Rain threatens, yet more photos,
Arches of flowers,
Organ legato,
Then trumpeting - they are here!
Father and daughter gilding the aisle,
Ebony and ivory tuned,
Their parting for our new son -
Vows are clear, the choir sings,
Tears fall fast but happy,
Processing to the voluntary.

Outside a deluge but no damp,
Our hearts are sunny and glow
As we greet old friends and family -
We sip, chatting, laughing and dine,
The speeches with thanks a blur,

Cake is cut, framed by flashes -
Then the first waltz,
The new partners
Leading the way to the next stage
And we follow, confident in love.

Stephanie Mottram

SCRUFF

Dear Friend,
It is nearly seven years since you came into my life,
and my life was turned upside down,
you came to me,
and at once I could see that
everything was going to be so very different.
Without a word or question said,
you climbed up quietly to my bed
and over the years I found a companion
that has asked no question of me
but who has missed me when I went away
yet still asked no more of me
than to come home to you,
after I would stray.

No wonder I can look into your eyes
not giving alibis, or looking for a prize.

There were times when you were ill
and I knew not how to comfort you, or whether
I would have to seek help for you, and
even wondered if you would be beside me
in the following morning.

I never needed to look up to you, for you were,
and still are, your own person; wanting but little
and giving so much, my cat for seven years
'Scruff'
I salute you!

A J Marchant

WHEN I'M WATCHING LITTLE CHILDREN

When I'm watching little children
And enjoying them at play
Absorbed in simple innocence
And loving what they say,
A thought brews up to haunt me
And make my conscience sore,
Are we leaving them a future
Without the threat of war?

When I look at what's around me
And I see the children's joy,
A sweet and charming innocence
The future could destroy,
I feel a pang of sadness
That the world's in such a state,
That good is marred by badness
Which has a root in hate:

I let my mind go wandering,
The children's glee goes on
It ends up with me wondering
Will one day it be gone?
And if it goes will in its place
Be happiness to spread
And help to heal the human race
Of hate in years ahead?

Nicholas Winn

THE ATTIC

An attic large with window high.
Shadows cast by moonlit sky.
Strange and angular shapes revealed.
Books and maps in parcels sealed.

Trunks of toys from far off days.
Packaged and wrapped in tidy ways.
A child of intent and enquiring mind.
Fashions of old - will in future find.

Tables and chairs of sturdy weight
Styled in carved and sculptured state.
Broken lamps and caskets bare
Hidden in dust and beyond repair.

Still intact - a baby's cradle
A remembered nursery rhyme and fable.
Green suede shoes of elfin size.
High black boots with hooks and eyes.

Old love letters tied with string.
In cotton wool - a tiny ring.
Long lost love of yesteryears
With recall is still held dear.

Memories happy - memories sad.
Finding a keepsake makes one glad.
Contemplating - as the sage
The pleasures of a gentle age.

Joy M Jordan

FRANCESCA

(A tribute to a bright 9 year old)

Francesca is a well-loved girl in Leigh,
with spelling and word knowledge unsurpassed,
equipped with attributes and memory;
with knowledge, for her age, that's simply vast.
Now, as she moves towards that magic 'ten',
we all feel pride in what she has achieved.
She's set herself a standard, regimen
whereby she must excel in every deed;
but never must she fail to satisfy
her aims, thus proving all her seriousness
to be the very best in all she'll try.
Unknown is failure: the one goal is success.
Francesca, you will always be our pearl;
stay young, have fun, enjoy, remain our girl!

Christopher Head

NEW DAD

There is a man who sings out heartily,
For the day is bright and the air is free;
Grasses and trees are strongly growing,
And warm west winds keep gently blowing,
And the glowing sun shines over all the land . . .
Creation rings with the song he sings exultantly,
Telling the world, all day long, of his glee!

The man is glad; sings it long and loudly;
Treats his friends to pints, and boasts proudly
About the one he loves who, last night,
Gave him a present which, in his sight
Overtones all the gifts he ever had or dreamed of . . .
A little girl, fair like Mum, who will soon make him glad
By boasting for years to come, 'He's my Dad!'

Dan Pugh

DAISIES ON THE DIAL

(Malone House Gardens - July 2000)

Granddaughter Katherine says that daisies,
From the downward-sweeping lawns above the
Tree-lined Lagan, are for The Birthday Girl!
(A role she relishes. All the year round!)
Twined with the odd buttercup, they're gathered
Willy-nilly, and heaped in my open
Hands before she begins her performance.
(Yet another rehearsal for her Fifth!)
Now, arms aloft, she twirls - and scatters them
Above the grey pavement at this little
Boxwood hedge - where I've found a welcome seat.

Like a votive off'ring for the altar
Of some ancient god, the airborne blossoms
Settle on this copper surface, etched in
Homage to the pathways of an antique
Sun. Sweet daisies on the dial of Time!

Their nectar, she's learned at Summer School, lies
Hidden within the yellow, central orb.
Yet, on the sun-warmed terrace behind us,
Outside the cool and stately rooms, they've set
The tables where a man-made Nectar of
The Gods will sparkle soon - quite openly -
To mark the taking of the marriage vows.

On some future days that shine like this, as
Heaven's Timeclock casts a measured shadow
On the daisy chain of Life, will she - and
Others who, like serenaded Daisy,
Have answered Yes nearby - bring children to
These quiet lawns? Perhaps to share again
A delight in simple things, and watch sweet
Daisies settle on a sun-drenched dial!

Stanley A McElroy

GRADUATION DAY

Your Graduation's here at last
And, though exams are long since past,
Today's the day we sing out loud,
Congratulations! We're so proud
Of everything that you've achieved,
For, through the years we've watched you weave
This tapestry, which is your life,
And, though you may find threads of strife,
They're oversewn with treasured pearls
So, when your tapestry's unfurled
You only see the happy days
Embroidered in a golden haze.
Feel proud as you don cap and gown,
You're now a person of renown!
As your diploma you collect,
Upon the years you will reflect -
You've worked so hard to reach your goal,
Now there's contentment in your soul;
So many special days you've shared
With people who have truly cared.
And may today be special too,
No one deserves it more than you.

Kay Spurr

CRY OF THE HEART

Nobody listens,
Nobody understands,
No one calls -
My name.

I need you,
Father,
Mother,
As the grass
Needs the rain -

To cover me
In your love -

To whisper in my ear,
'Do not cry,
Do not fear,

You mean -
Everything -
To me'.

Ken Price

OUR KID

He clambers out of cot at dawn
Not bothered that it isn't warm.
So full of vigour and feeling steadfast
In hot pursuit of early breakfast.

The noise he makes as woke up Mum
Who reaches for her precious son.
To hold and cuddle in her arms
The little one with all his charms.

Mum knows he wants his breakfast nosh
But not before he's had a wash.
He splashes out while in the bath
With such a hearty little laugh.

So fresh and clean with parted hair
He sits up in his breakfast chair
With dipped toast soldiers in his egg
So happy now and so well fed.

With such a smile on one so sweet
In loving hands with Mum to keep.
Protected, safe, and well cared for,
To cherish lovingly ever-more.

Michael Swain

GROWING AWAY FROM JESUS

Unless you believe as children do
You shall not enter in
You seek knowledge your whole life through
But the race you just can't win.

As a child you are close to God,
In his image you are created
But as through Satan's land you trod
Your holiness is dissipated.

Children believe so eagerly,
Never asking for proof or sign,
In a child God's spirit runs free,
Their innocence is quite divine.

Jesus said 'Let them come to me,
Do not hinder them at all,
For heaven belongs to such as thee'.
They are the foundation of heaven's walls.

To harm a child, you harm the Lord
And his father who sits on high,
Your life will be eternally flawed,
God will judge you this when you die.

As we are all brothers through Christ
So all children are our inheritance too,
All I can offer is this advice,
God created the Child - You created You!

Bill Hayles

TOMBOYS THROUGH AND THROUGH

Both of my beautiful daughters were terrible tomboys,
More interested in climbing trees than playing with toys.
Would stand up to anyone larger than them in a fight,
And then go on fighting if they thought they were right.

For the game of football, they both showed a genuine flair,
While their older brothers for football did not really care.
But of course with time passed they are all grown up and mature,
And both seem to have acquired a gentler female nature.

Though sometimes regarding them, I catch a look of regret,
Knowing given the chance they would still climb trees for a bet.

S Mullinger

THE LAZY SCARECROW

The farmer, and his dog searched high and low,
Through the orchard, and where the turnips grow,

Over the hills, where the sheep all graze,
And down in the valley among the maze,

All around the paddock, where the horses roam,
And into the stye, where the pigs call home,

Past the barn where they milk all the cows,
Across the fields that the farmer ploughs,

Around the pond where the ducks are quacking,
And into the yard where the geese are cackling,

Upon the meadow where all the rabbits play,
Till they find the lazy scarecrow sleeping in the hay.

Jim Cuthbert

MY FAMILY

Mark, Zoe and John the children that
I built my life upon,
They all look very different and are
Therefore not a copy carbon.

At six-feet tall a grey-eyed blond
My first son looks so good,
He can be very charming if he is in
A good mood.

Zoe at five-feet five of woman with
Nice auburn hair,
Has bright blue eyes that flash if
Things don't seem to be quite fair.

John at five-feet ten works hard
Upon his wood machine in a world
Of men.

His blue eyes came from vikings
In the past,
Up there our Scottish relatives
Made peace with them at last.

And his black hair from the Paisley Clan
Who came from Roman stock,
Means that the family's not a new kid on the
Block.

The many hardships we came through
At least we are alive,
It's good to see four grandchildren
Who really seem to thrive.

Jean Paisley

INNOCENCE

She was taking life in her stride
And she never seemed fazed.
I've never seen her jolted,
Just praised.
She's taking life as it comes
As she only should do
Never fussing
Just loving the days.

She's having trouble at night
I guess because she's so alive
She gets tired from putting
Herself on the line
But I guess this is better
Than a life of compromise
Not able to sleep
Because her life's on the line.

Naomi Elisa Price

YOUR MISSING SMILE

Child, please come to me, and tell me of your troubles
If you keep them locked inside, that way, the problem doubles
Don't forget, that I, was once a child like you!
And I'm sure I know, just what you're going through.

I see a sadness, in your face, it's been there for a while
Please, let me help you, find your missing smile
You're not the same sweet child, without your cheeky grin
Without that sunny smile, you're missing something from within.

Once, that laughing face, brightened up my day
Now eyes that danced with mischief rarely look my way
Life's road, I know, is fraught with joy and sorrow
Yet the pain we feel today, is often gone tomorrow.

I would like to take you, hold you in my arms
To comfort and console you, keep you safe from harm
But every time I speak you turn and walk away
Leaving me at a lose, as to what to do, or say.

The precious gift you had, has somehow gone astray
Who ever stole your laughter took the sunlight from your day
But with love, and understanding, from your Mum and me
I'm sure the way you feel, will soon be just a memory!

Karl Jakobsen

BIRTH

Eyes that sparkle and shine,
Second only to rays of sunlight,
Warmth, that of a mother's love,
Beauty, as of an angels presence,
Guardian of the giver of life.

Innocence, owned by all, but none,
At birth - given of a child,
The past married to the future,
As a gift from both, that of future life.

Moments, that pass faster than memories,
- Forever to remain -
But as of that, which was,
- Never to return -
Only when life chooses to share,
- With those of its own -
As giver, of its present, once again.

Bakewell Burt

JOCKWIN THE GOBLIN

This tale is about Jockwin the goblin
Which as you know is a tiny wee man
And he loves to practise his magic
As the very best goblins all can.

He lived deep in the green forest
In a fairy house by a stream
Happy and safe in the knowledge that
By humans he couldn't be seen.

When the local children came to play
And sometimes trample his fence to the ground
He'd get angry and to get his own back
Scare them off by making wild animal sounds.

Or he would magic the trees to reach out for them
As they ran here and there at their play
And as the branches would reach out and clutch at their legs
They'd scream in terror and run fast away.

As they would run in fear from the forest
He would chase them though they couldn't see
But they would hear his hysterical laughter
As he would caper and dance in his glee.

But then when the forest was quiet once more
And just the sound of the birds filled the air
He'd get lonely and long for a visit
Of the children that once more he could scare.

Don Woods

GRAND VIEW

Third grandchild born yesterday
resembles younger daughter
auntie to Zack.
As I'm told I'm like my maternal grandfather
whom I've never known -
although the story told
is that he took one look at me and died -
yet it's true in that he loved the countryside
walking and feeling the spirit
which is a thing that I love.
My younger daughter feels where people are
gets into the nub of their spirit, knows where they tick
wonder if my new grandson will
or what bit of the torch he will carry on
or light for him?

Sometimes we pass on a sort of truth,
or an agony, along with the love
a generation or two apart.

Robert D Shooter

TURN

Three seasons of travail are spent
It's time now for the big event
A slap, a cry, a bouncing boy
Has come to bring his parents joy.

Turn round but once; he's crawled away
Turn twice and he's a year today
Turn three times and he'll be ten
A man then, when you turn again.

As birthdays slide into the past
Each one comes quicker than the last
Your bouncing babe is now full grown
With bouncing babies of his own.

The pain and sorrow, fears and tears
Of parenthood's sweet poignant years
Are compensated by the love
Of bouncing blessings from above.

N G Charnley

LITTLE ANGELS

An angel, a cherub, a sleeping child
Or maybe two,
Can be found in the 'Old Masters' paintings
And sculpture too.
But in real life you can still see them
Embodied here,
For they exist in all little children
Far and near.
If you are fortunate enough to have
Children yourself,
You'd have seen often your child asleep
Innocence itself.
Who has not crept into the room at night
To take a peep.
And stopped to admire them laying
In sleep so deep.
So peaceful, quiet, clean and beautiful
Such a setting.
A reminder of angels and cherubs,
Of the paintings.

Terry Daley

NEW BORN

Round eyes that seek to focus on the world
Limped with trust, at the beginning of your life
Eager to meet the wonders that will be unfurled
Pandora's box revealing pain and grief and strife.

How will you meet the challenge of each passing day
The thousand paths of opportunity and scope
What can we offer, as you tread life's thorny way
But there through all will be the gentle hand of *hope.*

Alison Spencer

REFLECTIONS OF YOUTH

He looks in the mirror, he primps and he preens,
He's been acting like this since his early teens.
Three times a day he washes his hair
And sprays his deodorant with consummate care.
But his room is a tip, any time, day or night,
And he never remembers to turn off the light.
If he can't find his jeans, he will grumble and grouse,
But he leaves his possessions all over the house.
His manners at home are an utter disgrace,
But when with his friends, not a word's out of place.
His girl friend takes precedence now over all,
His life is committed to her beck and call.
All warnings on smoking he chose to ignore,
So his car has fag packets all over the floor.
He's a lodger without a lodger's concern,
And any advice from his parents he'll spurn.
In fact he's a typical 'youth of today',
And like all his peers wants to 'go his own way'.
Then one day maturing he'll wake from youth's dream,
And he'll realise just what a pain he has been.

D G Ives

TEENAGE BLUES

An apple a day keeps the doctor away
but what keeps those dreadful spots at bay.
Love makes the world go around,
crushes are certainly most profound.
Tears make your face most wet
is that what they call the hormone upset.
You have your very own ideological views
but parents never ever listen to you.
The imaginary increased weight gain,
life will simply never be the same.
Beauty is in the eye of the beholder,
no make-up until you are much older
In love with all the boys in your grade
is crushed when you are told about Aids.
A sly smoke behind the bike sheds,
Cancer you are told is the statistics of deaths.
Dreams of a white wedding with children too,
a short reminder cruelly curt first you must do homework.
What you think is really mean,
No alcohol until you are eighteen.
Though you may think your parents are not fair,
they do care and you they so love true,
You are a teenager just suffering the blues . . .

Diane Full

HERE TODAY . . .

Bill and coo,
Peek 'a boo,

Tongue-tied,
Sleepy-eyed,

Full of joy,
Daddy's boy,

Twinkle toes,
Runny nose,

Looks unhappy,
Change her nappy,

Sit and crawl,
Scream and bawl,

Dirty botty,
Needs a potty,

Mummy, Mummy,
Where's her dummy?

Down in dumps,
He's got the mumps,

Winter drizzle,
Teethe and grizzle,

Try and toddle,
It's a doddle!

Well I'll be blowed,
He's hit the road!
And who's this Larry
She wants to marry!?

Peter Davies

MY TREASURE, JENNIFER

The first time that I held you
You looked so very sweet
Then you smiled and stole my heart
You made my life complete
The months are going quickly
And you are growing fast
I hope that you remember me
And that our love will last
Then when I come to see you
A smile crosses your face
You toddle up to where I sit
We have a warm embrace
You are a little treasure
So sweet for all to see
I never will forget you
And please remember me
        Your loving granny.

Sheila Elkins

COMFORT LOVE

With arms so long and warm and gentle,
You hug me better when I'm sentimental.
You'll always be here to comfort me,
You never scold me for not eating my tea.
Hold me tight, I'll love you forever,
I won't forget you until we're together.
Daddy come back to me, I'm missing you so,
I'll cuddle your old cardigan and never let it go.

B S Allport

DOUBLE BLESSING

(Danielle and Louise Weeks. Born 5.9.99)

It started as an ordinary day
A sweet, fresh September morning.
To our joy, I found You had sent our way
Such a very special blessing.
From your loving heart, poured without measure,
You sent into our world that day,
Two new lives - it was a double treasure
They will bring us joy forever!

Two new lives, little girls so very small
Needing us to love and nurture,
To help and succour to grow strong and tall
In body, mind and spirit.
Our hearts are filled with love and grateful praise
For the wonder of creation.
And we worship our God, whose mighty ways
Are beyond our comprehension.

Mary Weeks

COMPARISONS

Years ago, I cared for a
puppy - and this is much
the same;
she scrambles at my feet
snuffling;
tugs at my skirt
whimpering;
circles in her bed
rustling;
chews at my hand
biting;
pulls at my shoe laces
playing;
runs after the cat
chasing . . .
then my baby smiles
enchantingly!

L A Churchill

VOWS OF LOVE

To have and to hold, for richer and for poorer,
These are the first vows of love.
To be able to take the rough with the smooth,
These are vows of love.
To never forsake the promises you make to each other,
These are vows of love.
To stand together against adversity when all seems lost.
These are vows of love.
As the bloom of youth begins to fade, but you only see the youthful
face.
These are vows of love.
When cross words are exchanged and you can forgive each other,
These are vows of love.
When the dreams you both first shared still hold vision,
These are vows of love.
And when the love you share reaches into the lives of others,
Then these are the truest vows of all.

Carol Holmes

THOSE HAPPY DAYS

I well remember the days we had to go outside even for a drink,
For facilities included merely an outhouse, with a boiler and
    a sink.
There was only a cold tap and so to bathe was quite an ordeal.
To look back on those days some would hardly believe that it was
    real.
The toilet was in a party yard, and we even had to share,
For in terrace houses to have an individual toilet was very rare.
In fact, many toilet facilities consisted of just a hole in the ground,
And all this would be taken care of when what were known as
    night soil men, came around.
The coal fired boiler provided hot water, when to take a bath we
    had to use a tub,
And the same boiler would be used to wash clothes when there'd
    be the need to scrub.
Despite all of the discomfort, our family was happy and content,
And there'd be some job we'd find to do, in order to survive,
    that's how the day was spent.
Then came the war years, when we had to adjust our belt.
It was an ounce of this, and perhaps none of that, when hardships
    we all felt.
But there was camaraderie, no time to envy others.
We'd share our last morsel, they were regarded as our sisters
    and our brothers.
Where did it all go wrong, to lead to what we have today?
There's unmitigated cruelty and lack of respect in every way.
No one would like to see the return of what we had to contend
    with in the past.
But if everyone was forced to be responsible for their own affairs,
    perhaps we'd get peace at last.

Reg Morris

GRATITUDE

Gratitude springs from the inner being,
It comes from the depths of the soul.
Light words of thanks slip off a glib tongue
As an actor when playing a role.

Real gratitude brings all love in its train
When the giver has given with pleasure.
Gratitude then relives that joy
And returns love without measure.

Pettr Manson-Herrod

JUST A PHONE CALL AWAY

Snowdrift skies
And ice blue eyes
Sweet midnight
Lullabies
Empty morns
Unshared the dawns
Your telephonic
Sighs

Bitter sweet
This lover's heat
A howling
At the moon
And hunger fed
On this cold bed
From empty
Honey spoon.

Kim Montia

SWITZERLAND REVISITED

It was so special returning here again.
We had our honeymoon in Switzerland
Just over 15 years ago.
Now we've had the chance
To come here once again,
This time with our two children -
James who is 8 and Paul aged 4.
The weather was glorious,
The scenery magnificent
Nothing else can compare
With this for mountains and fresh air!

We took a boat across the lake,
Then a train from the town of Interlaken,
Alighting at the pretty village of Wilderswil
Where we had spent such happy days
At the start of our marriage.
We strolled past the little weather station
Where people stop to look at the barometer,
We showed our sons the hotel where we stayed -
It hadn't changed.
Even the troughs with the drinking fountains
Were just the same . . .
And the familiar sound of the cowbells
Resounding over the fields.

Cathy Mearman

A SPECIAL TIME - FRIEND
(Beloved Sandy dog)

Thoughts of a special time
Ascending today
Passed in the senses
Directing my prayer
I observed with obedience
Dynamics of breeze
Studied movement of nature
Ever flowing - at ease
Sun glow while radiating
Warmth on my face
Illuminated lips
Where fell silently 'Grace'
In a requisite moment
Of melodizing blend
Philomel sang of reunion
Blessed a special time - friend.

Irene Gunnion

THERE IS A LITTLE CORNER

There is a little corner by the garden wall,
When I was a young child
I played with bat and ball,

There is a little corner by the garden wall,
Where first I met my true love,
Oh! So handsome, straight and tall,

There is a little corner by the garden wall,
And there I had my first kiss,
My heart with love so full!

There is a little corner by the garden wall,
Where I take our children,
To play . . . and stories . . . to recall.

There is a little corner by the garden wall,
I come to sit, in its shade.
My tears on it, to fall.

There is a little corner by a garden wall,
Now my love it holds within
And only . . . shadows fall . . .

Sylvia Connor

JULIE'S 21ST BIRTHDAY

So many years since you were just a baby in my arms
Not worrying, nor caring who fell unto your charms.
You enchanted so many people then, simply with a smile,
For charm you had no rivals - a winner by a mile.
And 'though you are so grown-up now you have not lost your touch,
As I did then, so I do now. I love you very much.

J G Ryder

SLEEP SOUNDLY SWEET BABE

Sleep soundly sweet babe under your blanket of stars
For morning will bring all your little heart desires
Innocent as yet 'ere the years take their toll
Snug in your cot as you gurgle and roll.

Time enough in a decade for the pressure to tell
School and exams'll almost certainly be hell
Man-cub you must arm yourself good
For life's competition, it's as regular as food.

When you become a full man you'll worry that girls
May not 'dig' much your charm if you haven't got curls
Enough cash, and a job'll take up most of your time
Perhaps, if you're lucky, you'll find a wife who's sublime.

The rearing of kids could well be a pain
Many times you will say - 'Oh never again!'
The mortgage, the bills, and all of that stuff
Will be bound to set you off in a huff.

If you make it to mid years relatively clear
You'll be lucky, for now you'll have little to fear
Just hang on to your health, you'll be quids in you bet
It's a priceless commodity - one you must never forget.

In the autumn of life now, all should be serene
For it's little use thinking of what might have been
Your memory-bank should be full of good powers
So sleep soundly sweet babe under your blanket of stars.

Paul Harvey Jackson

JANE

Wrapped within
  an angelic shroud
you sat;

Your eyes like sapphire stars
  sparkling
in the cool midnight sky;

Your hair burning
  red
like the hot desert sun;

Your skin as
  soft
as a birth of rose petals;

And your lips
  sweeter
than the sweetest nectarine;

And from that first moment
  I looked into your eyes
smiling back at me, I knew
  you would be mine.

Marc Tyler

OUT OF THE BLUE

The in's and out's of Mondays, an early start, away,
School to Perton shopping, then the town bank, starts the day.
So far down the agenda, the thought of cheques, 'No stop!'
Back home to fetch the rent cheque sets our phone a ringing off.

'Early to central office, can you come on your combo?
Your motorbike and sidecar's been requested for a show.'
Astonishing change for Wednesday, BBC2's the fact,
Wish to film our BSA beauty that backfires with such a crack.

Entitled, 'From The Edge' is the programme, Tuesday's shown,
Filming converted bikes for disabled on the road,
Our good old fashioned combo, self converted, eighty-one,
Aside the charities adapted, shows great help since they began.

My descriptions must be 'gobsmacked' or 'flabbergasted trance'
As the phone met the receiver and bewilderment the glance.
Gren's inner self lay fainted in a splatter on the floor,
'The first of March, this Wednesday;' He could register no more.

A magic time upon that day, enjoyment all around
With six members of the filming crew, not forgetting light and sound.
Engrossed in fun and laughter, sure a day to reminisce,
Worth the hardy ride to Stockport, the presenter worth the kiss.

Sara Russell, Golden Eagles MCC

MY SPECIAL TIMES

In my mind is a special place
Where memories are stored
Memories of my special times
When I was never bored.

Memories of my schooldays
Of days when I was young
Playing games, flying kites
To me they were such fun.

Memories of the rainforests
And the creatures that within them bred
Soon there will be no rainforests
And all the creatures will be dead.

My special times mean so much to me
Full of dreams and memories
Special times spent with special friends
Halcyon days I wished would never end.

Nothing will ever make me
Forget my special times
In my heart they will always stay
Remembered fondly every day.

Special times, special faces
Special memories, special places
It isn't often that you find
Special times of a special kind.

D Linnett

THE PICNIC

A ritual organised by those near and dear
Where cousins, aunts and uncles, join us once a year.
It was a special day to picnic in our favourite place
High up on Dartmoor, to sit, walk or race
With balls, kites, a cricket bat and such,
All the family gathered, we loved it so much.
We packed the pasties and the pies, the jam puffs and some fruit,
Trudging o'er the heather with contents of car boot.
Over streams and rocky humps, boxes rattled with the bumps,
Aunty June brought all the drink, you should have heard her bag clink.
We found a patch of level ground to place a chair for Gran
Who always came, she was game, and enjoyed her noisy clan.
All were happy, even Dad who usually had a moan
About anything and everything, sometimes we wished he stayed at
Home,
Today it was perfect, sunshine with a breeze,
It sent the kites up high and low, so quick the wind a constant tease.
We ate the food with relish, appetite's keen when in fresh air,
Dad found time to sketch the scene, for that he had a flair.
We laughed, we joked, we played our favourite games,
When tired sat in a ring and played the one spelling names.
Time soon went, all were spent, of energy to play,
Packing our gear to all it was clear it had been a perfect day.
Homespun and simple, surely, this is how it ought to be,
As I look at my happy family, I am pleased I am me.

Patricia Evans

SEASONS OF LIFE

Childhood dreams are ones to treasure,
Just the kind which last forever.
They're of the season known as spring,
When we think we're sure of everything.

Life is harder when summer comes,
We have to work and do our sums.
Living the rat race is not much fun,
But alas, it has to be done.

When autumn comes we're often tired,
Perhaps! we think, we should retire.
After all we've done our best
For others, and deserve a rest.

We soldier on through winter days,
It becomes a struggle in so many ways.
Stretching a pension isn't much fun,
But, somehow we manage and the battle is won.

Val Bermingham

THE WONDER OF A CHILD

Gazing, exquisite, the child
Sits and looks,
Surveying the jumble of toys,
Sweets and books.
Sitting around the Christmas tree,
With brothers and sisters,
Her family.
There I saw beauty,
No flaw spoiled the grace
That flowed from the look
On that innocent face.
Happiness, contentment
And sheer delight.
The wonder of a child,
On Christmas night.

Katrina M Anderson

A Day Of Summer Stored

A summer day,
Rare and beautiful,
Walking through harebells,
High on fresh air.

Moors with heather,
Then at the roadside,
A caterpillar,
Hairy and brown.

In case of cars,
Coaxed it with a stem,
Round which the creature,
Curled happily.

She placed this on,
The green grass verge,
That is her way with,
Small helpless things.

All summer caught,
In memory stored,
Of a special day,
With a daughter.

Kathleen M Scatchard

FELIXSTOWE PROMENADE

Canned noise versus washed woven rhythm
clanking coarse choruses of lines of
sanctified slot machines
that call worshippers to offer
their tokens in the hope of reward
which they return forthwith to their noisy idols.

Away from this the breeze plays games
with cheeky seagull wind surfers.
Brave families make castles of stone and sand
sheltering and trying to hide from the wind's cool caress.
The glaring noise of the arcade fades as
we wander along the paved promenade
the waves rushing up to the beach take over the music stand
with softer yet harsher tones -
the scent of sea salt, seaweed and Suffolk.

The desire to get close to hear and feel the
waves, as they rush headlong determined to invade the land
but sulking fall back repelled.
People are well covered now as the open landscape
contrives with the wind to wreck hairstyles and remove head coverings.
We walk further, drinking in the autumn air, enjoying the battle
between sea and land, wondering at this foaming freshness
preparing to savour our fish and chips.

Tony McLarty

PRECIOUS ROSEBUDS

Yous are my little rosebuds with lips of petal pink
With cheeks that are all rosy red and noses autumn mink
With heads so fair and bright snow white with eyes carnation blues
With eyebrows like those leaves of brown that's what I think of yous.
Your skin's so soft and peachy cream, your voice's sweet and tender
Your hands are soft and yet so small, your fingers long and slender
And when I watch yous out at play I cannot help to see
Of all the things you're made up of yous are made so perfectly.
I love you all so dearly, yous mean the world to me
Yous are my precious rosebuds and you will always be.

> There will never be anyone so important in my life, as
> important in my life as yous, yous are angels sent from heaven
> to light up my life and give my world a special meaning.

Deborah Elizabeth Gorman

AUDLEM

Have I been here before?
Canal locks look the same.
Midland salt town, village -
Is this where I came?

So many summer holidays
Spent on the waterways!
Someone else walked in my shoes
In those distant days.

Now I walk on the muddy tow-path,
Bright glow the berries here,
But brown the canal water
Though the sky is blue and clear.

The chugging long boats pass me
In autumn's red and gold.
Audlem! I do remember -
The memories unfold

Of a time that I have lived through
And yet as over and done
As ancient civilisations
Once proud beneath the sun.

Youth had aspirations,
But middle years are kind
And there's no going back there,
No solutions to find.

Words are elusive,
Don't express how I feel.
Could one but grasp a past
Made tangible, made real!

Nostalgia's a luxury and
Pleasurable the pain somehow
As I stroll in the sunshine
Of Audlem here and now . . .

Jacqueline Abendstern

DARK BLUE DUSK

A pink purple hue
Covers the sky.
The birds silently
Flutter by.
Only a quiet chirp and twitter
Is heard from afar.
The heat is stifling and clammy,
Although a small breeze
Gently blows through the trees;
Ruffling the leaves
Whilst sending cherry blossom
Whirling and twirling to the ground.
Soon, there isn't a sound.
The pink purple hue
Turns dark blue,
The stars begin to appear,
The dark blue
Turns slowly black
And the night is still.

Lesley-Ann Curdy

YOU ENCOURAGED US

Thank you Sue Hopton for what you've done
Although it was serious stuff we had some fun,
How to sharpen our listening skills
How to see body signs and concentrate still,
What to look for and how to look for signs
And to sometimes know when to read between the lines,
Pastoral care is serious stuff but now we know
That the signs we give out can help us show,
That we are being attentive to what's being said
And know how and when to comfort if tears are shed,
The time we shared was for us well spent
And I think you really were heaven sent,
You told us to know our limitations too
And to give it to God who has a better view,
I hope this little poem will encourage you
Just as much as you encouraged us few,
I think that we all want and deserve
More of these lessons on how to serve,
Also when our time with people we share
Let's pray they know that we listen and care.

George Reed

FIRST LOVE

Though more than half a century has passed
since we walked hand in hand through summer grass,
the picture of that scene will always last . . .
colours still bright.
The sighing of the wind through drying hay.
Impressions of our bodies as we lay
somnolent in heat of summer day,
in filtered light.
The cornflowers as blue as were your eyes.
The scarlet poppy petals round us lie.
My pulse has palpitations and I sigh . . .
all things just right.
The fertile smell of foliage and soil.
The tickly touch of clover and trefoil.
The buzzing of the insects as they toil.
Clouds high and white.
As you leaned towards me, time stood still.
Your lips touched mine and woke an adolescent thrill.
Sweet memory that will stay with me until
Life's final night.

Ida Shewan

LOVE

Love is a strange old condition,
It grabs, as you part from your date
That first time, becoming a mission
In seconds, and then it's too late.

It's with you first thing in the morning,
It's there as you open your eyes,
It gnaws at the conscious while scorning
All sense, by the foolish or wise.

It feeds on the hidden emotions,
It puffs itself up into truth,
It desires all manner of potions,
And in proving itself, is uncouth.

It gets you at gainful employment,
On a platform or underground train,
It speeds past contented enjoyment,
And makes you feel madly insane.

It's tangible, but then it's intangible,
It behaves as a will o' the wisp,
It encourages behaviour so laughable,
Consuming in fires to a crisp.

It's sometimes there when you want it,
But it's quite often mistaken for lust,
It grows when you try not to feed it,
And when fed, often crumbles to dust.

Unrequited it causes obscenity,
Changing life, in a sad bitter twist,
But requited, it takes on serenity,
When embraced, and when fondled and kissed.

Rupert Buryan

KISS!

I watched across a crowded room
And glimpsed a golden moment
The chiselled features of your face
Etched on evening shadows
Laughter spilling from your eyes
Warmth, radiating round.
I slowly wandered round the room
Attraction, like a magnet
Reeling me in with practised precision
Compelled, no will, conform.
I couldn't help, but notice them
The others by your side
The charismatic flame oozed out
It emanated pride
As I came up to your side
Your laughter caught my eyes
You drew me close, protecting me
Your kiss caressed my brow
Without a word we turned to leave
And as you took my arm
I reached to kiss your wizened cheek
And with that touch convey
How much I'll always care for you, Dad
Each and every day.

Cate Campbell

MOONBEAMS AND KISSES

Towards my heart the faint nocturnal glimmers of
refracted moonlight travelled an infinite space.
Once there it instilled, nurtured, facilitated a feeling
of awe, a realisation of our Creator's eternal love.
That too of my beloved.

Moonbeams shining in her hair, twinkling in her eyes,
the corners of her mouth, in her every turn and twirl.
Reflecting, dancing, rejoicing about her as she entranced
me, leading me through the still, summer, midnight air.
Her full red pouty lips, accentuated and illuminated.
Perhaps a purse to keep sweet words from falling out
involuntarily.
Her kiss a foretaste of much fancier things to come
once familiar, pure fantasy.
The very essence of pure purpose and love.

The fine pleats of her evening gown, like mountain rivulets.
Her ultra-light step, not disturb no blade of grass, nor wing
of cricket or fine garb of illusive moth.
Her facial contours a representation of the angelic -
a voice like mesmerism, sirens calling.

Will she reveal tonight her ultimate intention to remain
in my inferior arms
or does she move like the fair, place-to-place never
settling anywhere.
Like the diffusion of the smell of candyfloss, popcorn and
toffee apples to other men's nasal receptors
or is she like those moonbeams, distant then temporarily
near and bright
Like moonbeams.

Dean T Axford

CRUSHING

Crushing and critical
That's what it feels like
Dangerous, exciting but wrong.
I want to do what's right
But these feelings are so strong
Making me curse my mind,
My secret places.

Punishing and painful
That's what it feels like.
Falling into the trap
Again, again, again
It's a form of torture
And ends up a form of self loathing.

Waves of uncertainty,
That's what it feels like.
A creeping, crawling longing.
To remain silent
To hold on and not let go
To read between the lines and
Get it so miserably wrong.

Lightyear

UNTITLED

Oh what bliss is a beautiful kiss,
It sends you straight to heaven.
His gentle arms around you, holding you tight,
Two hearts beating as you reach the heights.
His lips touching yours, soft and gentle is his kiss,
You go into a dream state, 'Oh' such bliss.
The blood rushes to your head, your body all a tingle,
You want to stay like this forever, let your passion mingle.
Your senses are reeling with this wonderful feeling,
You never want it to end.
Your heart still pounding, beautiful music sounding,
All these feelings abounding.
From the most melting sensation, the beautiful kiss,
The kiss, the kiss, 'Oh' bliss.

E Hughes

THE KISS

Gazing into eyes so true,
With eyes of love
Taking in your beauty and perfection.
Sitting near, yet so far,
Hearts joined,
Minds in total harmony.
Deep desire to touch,
Love reaching out,
Not the moment, can't interrupt.
At last the moment comes,
Lips brush, and meet
And melt with the passion of your embrace.

P Merrill

IN LOVE

The sun goes down amidst a blaze of light,
And once again, I'm lonely in the night,
The moon comes high, gives off its silver gleam,
I see your face in every glancing beam.

The beach is dark, but silver gleams the sea,
Oh! How I wish that you were here with me,
Together we would wander hand in hand,
Or lie together on the silver sand.

To talk of love, and with each sweet caress,
The lord above would seem to smile and bless,
This puny man, this mortal for a day,
T'would seem, he'd placed a rose upon my way.

For me to find, to cherish to my heart,
To hold so close, and never more to part.
Then when the Day of Judgement comes,
To answer for my living,

I'll answer, 'Lord, I've never been,
Outside the Gates of Heaven'.

Robert Simpson

MEMORY OF LOVE

Memory of love, you are painful!
I must sing and burn in your smoke,
But for others - you're just a flame to
Warm a cooling soul.

To warm a sated body, they needed my tears . . .
For this I received love's communion!
Let me drink some kind poison
That will make me mute . . .
And turn my infamous fame into
Radiant oblivion.

Siobhan Fox (15)

IN A KISS

Two sweet lips to comfort a tear as it falls
A little love from the lips on a child's cheek
A quick, soft touch with a smile of happiness on a face.

So sweet is a kiss, just a gentle little kiss
A kiss that can say so much whatever your age
Compassion, comfort love
So much is in a kiss.

Jenny Johnson

HIS FIRST KISS

It's been a long wait,
For that moment of bliss;
My mates have all had it,
That illusive first kiss.

So many times,
It has nearly occurred;
Eyes closed, lips puckered,
Then there is heard;

A mischievous giggle,
A whispered excuse;
Back to the drawing board;
Lips on the loose.

But that's in the past now,
No need to grieve;
I'm surrounded by women,
Who can't even leave.

So who shall I choose,
In this grand Sunshine Home?
Time to get ready,
Might just use a comb;

I'll polish my false teeth,
'Til they're done to a tee;
It's that moment of magic,
For Doris and me.

M Cleasby

KISS

I'll kiss your lips,
Whenever I can.
Your beauty would move
Any man.

That kiss I stole from you,
All that time ago
Was the one thing, I'm sure,
That made our love grow.

So to kiss you now,
After all this time,
Is a gentle reminder
That you're still mine.

So let's keep on kissing,
All the time,
A soft reminder,
That our kissing will last the test of time.

Richard Sharpe

A Kiss

Take one second, a moment in time,
To remember something,
That taste, sweeter than wine,
Starting slowly, growing strong,
Wanting it to last, forever long,
Sweet desires from within,
Always wanting it to begin.
From starting young to growing old,
Worth more than its weight in gold.
A beautiful thing, full of desire
A burning passion, full of fire.
A wonderful thing, always desired so much,
A kiss can only happen
When two lips touch.

Steven Coates

KISSES

What is a kiss . . .
There are little kisses, soft, and dreamy
Kisses, and tender kisses,
Also kisses of passion, and desire,
When lovers, each other, admire,
Kisses of fondness, and kisses for caring,
A small, and tiny kiss,
When you say, you are leaving,
A dreamy kiss for your lover,
When you feel a little daring,
Tender kisses come from
Our grandmothers,
To show us the right of way,
There are kisses to mean kindness,
To be trustworthy, when we pray,
With kisses of affection,
When we give thanks,
To our Lord up above,
So we turn to our partner,
And kiss the one we love . . .

John A Shaw

THAT FIRST KISS

The increased beating of the heart,
Nerves abound,
- Wanting to get it right,
Not knowing which side to turn your
Head . . .
Boom!
Before you realise it
- You're kissing!
Enjoying it - all worries cast aside,
Nothing else matters.
Time itself eludes you,
Tingling from head to toe,
Never wanting it to end.
And, it never does.
Even years later you'll remember
That feeling of weightlessness,
- That special moment
Forever in your heart
That first kiss.

K O'Connor

YOUR LIPS

I love when you kiss
These lips of mine
Soft and warm as they
Entwine

Melting my heart with
Passion and fire
My eyes light up with
Warmth and desire

Kisses running down
My skin
With passions stirring
Deep within

Your lips they kiss my
Very soul
This moonlit night as we
Stroll.

Marilyn Davidson

LETTER TO MY MASTER

Dear Sir
I want to feel your hands on my body
I want to taste your lips on my mouth
I am longing for you like a junkie
I have fallen for you down and out

My mind's wild with desire
You can have me however you want
I need to feel you in me
You're my Master, I'm your servant

I am trembling with anticipation
Your breath on my neck is a thrill
You drive me mad with desperation
I am totally subject to your will.

Naked on my knees before you
Tears streaming down my face
Please, oh please don't say I bore you
Take me, kiss me.

Yours always

Miranda

LIPS

Lips are for kissing and caressing
Lips are for moving and expressing.
When you smile your lips turn up
When you frown your lips turn down.
Everything you eat goes through them
Everything you say goes through them.
Or are they there to stop you saying
Oh dear my mouth is fraying.
I still believe that lips are there
For kissing and caressing.

David Hamey

OBSERVED

Ugly
Awkward
Who should wish to touch
Such
A face?
But he
Longingly
Kisses with eyes
And she
Shyly
Responds with eyes
And love grows
Visible in eyes
And those
Two
Are alone
Surrounded
Together
And she
Loved
Into beauty.

Phil Fenton

SHE'S SO GREAT

She's so great, I'm totally in awe,
I can't find the bottle, to knock on her door.
I really need to tell her, how I feel
Or she'll never know that she's part of my deal.

I always see her around, I don't think she knows,
But what if she did, how would it go?
Maybe I'll tell her, the day after next,
Or in a week, a month at best.

Honest, I'll do it, I'll find the inspiration,
The courage, the spur, to make a visitation,
I'll knock on her door to make a date,
And that's when I'll tell her
That she's so great.

William Forrest

THE KISS

Anticipating your reaction, with baited breath I wait
Trying to steal that perfect moment
Before it becomes too late
All my life I've waited
From childhood until now
Wondering how you'd feel
If I stole that moment now.

All the times we've shared together
All the bad times
All the bliss
And now I dare, to risk it all
Just to steal a kiss.

Steve Moon

ZEST FOR LIFE

Boys and girls arms atwine,
Softly saying be mine, be mine.
Love is all around, or so people say,
But I wish some would come my way.
Love affairs they come and go,
Oh, how I miss that feeling so,
Being alone is such an ordeal,
You have to learn once more, to love, to feel,
That lovely warmth of someone new,
But it exists only in my mind's view.

That was me not so very long ago,
Feeling left out, alone, abandoned so.
But now my zest for life is so high,
I've been found by this, oh, so gorgeous guy!
One that treats me oh, so very good,
To be treated how a woman should.

Love comes to us all at some time,
Age difference really isn't a crime.
It's how you feel when love is around,
The zest for life once more has been found.
Especially when your first love has up and gone,
And you really thought 'he was the one'.
So I thank my lucky stars each new day,
That this perfect love has come my way.

C A Hartland

SWEET CHARITY

It was night, it was lonely when I walked into her street,
She said, 'Hello boy would you like the chance to meet?'
I've a million stories to sell you and a thousand dreams to weep,
For you're just another casualty in the war between the sheets.
And her name was Charity, giving faith and hope again to me,
Yes, her name was Charity, and Love was just another name for she,
Sweet Charity!

Rainbows, frogs and sausage men were games we liked to play,
But now they hide the memories of the girls who've gone astray.
Stacks of fading photographs, love letters carved in sand,
Dreams they came so easily when this lady took my hand.

Once upon a long dark night the world was at my feet,
Feeling like a Kings of Hearts with this lady o' so sweet.
But daybreak dawns too swiftly and reflected in her eyes,
I saw all the other men who listened to her lies.

Now I laugh and joke about the games we used to play,
And wallow in nostalgia for those days so far away.
Those days of Charity, giving faith and hope again to me,
Yes, her name was Charity, and Love was just another name for she,
Sweet Charity!

C N Messenger

THE ROSE

Oh my darling, the sweet smell of a rose,
Is the sweet aroma of you.
Ah such sweetness never have before to behold
The petals of the rose reminds me
Of your beauty you know.
And the bee that pollinates the rose,
Reminds me of all those sweet kisses
We have shared
And the leaves of the rose remind me
Of all the hugs we have shared
And the thorns are not sharp at all,
They remind me of the pins that
Hold up your golden hair
And the rose will keep on blooming
From year to year
Just as our love has for over 50 years.

Caprice Cappinceno

THE BLACKBIRD (A WAKING DREAM)

Dawn, and light slowly discovers
The unvarnished wood
And deep greenery that lives
In this quiet, scented room.

In the space between slumber
And awareness, I can feel
Your hair, its luxuriant darkness
Resting on my cheek and shoulder.

My arm rises and falls
Around your waist as you breathe
Soft and warm beside me
Wrapped in a mantle of peace.

Sunlight falls upon your hand,
Uncurling against old cotton.
'Listen, love, the blackbird.'
And sleeping still, you smile.

And draw me closer.

Louise Warrington

FIRST KISS

My first kiss was quite funny,
With tingles and jingles all over my body.
Holding hands up a tree,
We closed our eyes and wriggled close together,
With arms around each other, our lips came
Together and touched.
His lips were soft like marshmallow texture,
Wanting to bite through the soft interior.
Then our tongues collided, slimy and squidgy,
Wet and wiggly like a worm.
Our tongues went around like a fairground ride.
Grinding teeth catching together like a piece
Of sandpaper and that was my first kiss and that
Was something to remember.

Clare Satterthwaite

SO MANY KISSES

'Please marry me,' he murmured,
As they sat there, side by side.
Her face aglow, she answered.
'Yes, I will be your bride.'
He bent his head toward her,
And kissed her tenderly.
Then they talked and made their plans.
How happy they would be.

The day that they were married,
He kissed her once again.
And they kept on kissing,
Through sunshine and through rain.
Soon, she told him shyly,
'There's a baby on the way.'
They kissed in celebration
It was such a happy day.

One day she sat with babe in arms
Her husband by her side,
He said, 'I'll never rue the day,
I took you for my bride.'
Then they kissed their baby, son
While stars shone up above.
Their kisses are forever,
A symbol of their love.

Elizabeth Finlayson

SEVENTH HEAVEN

Oh love they say is King of Kings
A many splendoured thing
A hug, a kiss, exchange of rings
Oh what joy this can bring

The gentle art of loving charm
Eyes meet across a room
A gentle word - a loving glance
They meet - they kiss - the rest is bliss

The lips are red and hold a smile
Whilst arms are open wide
They hug, they cuddle just a while
And God is on their side

A kiss can mean so many things
Hello, goodbye - or heaven
Just tilt the head and bend the knee
And slowly count to *seven.*

C Goldsmith

A NORTHERN LAD

I saw him there at my last college ball,
With a sprig of mistletoe as I recall,
And he said he'd save his last kiss for me;
I replied that I'd wait and see!
For he was a Northern lad with a soul of fire,
The flames danced in his eyes -
And no matter how far we stood apart,
The attraction was hard to disguise.
As the evening passed I tasted kisses so sweet,
Some burned like brandy taken neat!
Some were merely a peck on the cheek;
But there were only two lips I yearned to seek!
Until finally I found him on the dance floor,
But then revellers swept him through the door,
So that gone forever was my only chance -
Yet I'll always remember his parting glance.
I never again saw that Northern lad,
But it was the best kiss I never had;
An embrace that promised such sweet surprise -
Was the kiss that burned for me in his eyes!

Akkeber Osborne

PRIVATE MOMENTS

Inspiration, beauty, elegance and class,
These things won't leave her as time goes past.
I steal private moments to gaze upon her face,
Her skin so pure like silken lace.

To pinch myself as I sometimes do,
I find it hard to believe, almost untrue
That this vision of beauty could be mine,
I hope forever our hearts entwine.

To *feel* so much can be flawed,
To let her know she's so adored.
But I'm not ashamed of my undying loyalty,
I will always see her as the highest royalty.

Martin Benson

LOVE
(For Jennifer Freeston Macdonald)

There is a light that encompasses all.
Understands the frailty of our souls.
Dwells in a stillness that knows no bounds.
Ascends, and descends.
Is present in this piercing moment,
And in the void of eternal infinity.
It is here in life, and in death.
Within the known, and unknown universe;
Its height, its length, its depth, and breadth.
Far out beyond the stars it soars;
Its omnipresent presence, stirs and boils.
In every beginning, in every end.
Around every twisting corner, bend.
On mountains high, and valleys deep.
Whilst wide awake, or in sound sleep.
It knows no bars or bolted doors.
Its light will last forevermore.
         'It is all that life's worth living for;'
Ingrained, ordained;
An immutable law;
         'Love!'

Nigel Gatiss

MOUTH TO MOUTH

I pulled back the covers right over my face
Thought of last night - was I in disgrace?
I'd never done anything quite so daring
As the 'kiss' that he and I were sharing.

Wartime Britain, romance everywhere
'Casablanca' time what did we care
This young Canadian sweet talkin' me
Canada on his sleeve - RCEME.

We kissed and caressed much in love were we
But I never succumbed my virginity . . .
An old lady now just reminiscing?
Not on your life!
I'm still up for kissing . . .

Pearl Johnston-Stewart

FIRST KISS

I'd swooned and swooned for the boy next door
Each time I saw him my emotions soared
And then one day my prayers were answered
When he asked to take me to the pictures.

He slipped his arm around the seat
And pulled me close - oh what a treat!
My dreams fulfilled and on cloud seven
Just one kiss and I'd be in heaven.

Hand in hand 'neath the stars we walked
Entwined together at my door we talked
When all at once from up the stair
My gran in nightie with curlered hair
Demanded that I get inside
No kiss for me - he ran off to hide!

June Fyfe

LOVE OF YOUR KISS

The taste of your kiss still lingers so strong
No feeling like this could ever be wrong
Sensations intense yet so carefree and wild
Are drowning my senses with magic beguile

Like a dream I go through the motions each day
Remembering your touch every word that you say
Heart chained emotions passionately wild
Long to be free yet stay secret inside.

The hands on the clock move too slowly for me
Impatient to see you I silently plea
As the day wanders on my confidence wanes
Is this real love or heartache and pain.

Then as I remember the love in your kiss
My heart cries a river drowning in bliss
How could I doubt the love in your kiss
No treasure in the world is as precious as this.

Mary O'Hara

KISS ME NOW

Kiss me love
Don't be afraid to kiss me
Kiss me now
For heaven's sake don't be so shy
Don't wait 'til time has passed us by
Yeah, you can do it if you try
Kiss me love
Kiss me now

Kiss me love
It ain't a crime to kiss me
Kiss me now
Let me be your reason why
Your all embracing alibi
For us the rules do not apply
So kiss me love
Kiss me now

Kiss me love
Just press your lips on mine and kiss me
Kiss me now
No matter what the stars may say
Before the skies have turned to grey
And all the wine has run away
Please kiss me love
Kiss me now

Rod Trott

BACKGROUND

Before you turn, give up, and walk away,
Recount the spring, the songs of May,
Remember the smell of pollen rich air,
The gentle touch on lovers hair,
Just weeks ago.

Has it brought back those remembered days?
The start of summer the morning haze,
Alive with hope and longing to share,
Those blissful moments without a care
Just days ago.

It has?
That kiss, those lingering thoughts,
It happened just passed that fearful pause,
When eyes are closed but minds still race,
To reach that Love, that mutual place,
Just hours ago.

The wonderful journey through Heaven and space,
That accompanies your thoughts, your dearest ones face,
Indelibly etched but publicly showing,
The World can see, you're outwardly glowing,
Just minutes ago.

Now stop. And breathe. Look into those eyes,
There's feeling in there, why believe lies,
Give it all up, throw it away,
For something that's said in the heat of the day?
Just seconds ago.

Ian Phillips

LOVE AND LOVE OF THE KISS

Love lies sleeping in our souls
It stirs and then it rises
Love can bloom in many ways
It's full of sweet surprises
The magic and the mystery
Can lead your heart astray
Love captures you within its spell
And deepens day by day.

When you fall deeply into love
You'll feel sweet joy and pain
It warms you with its sunshine
Then cools you with its rain
Passion filled kisses, full of desire
Enchant you, on and on
Promises whispered of undying love
That you build your dreams upon.

Love can be the comfort felt
Among our dearest friends
Our brother's and our sister's love
We cherish and defend
Love should be forsaken not
It's special from the start
Love bears our emotions
It's the keeper of our hearts.

A father's love floats endlessly
His kiss is full of pride
The greatest idol to the child
His love he cannot hide,
This strength will carry with them
And journey through the years
From youth until eternity
He shields their darkest fears.

Her love remains our kingdom
The golden memories that we keep
She gently chased our tears away
With kisses tender sweet
She's a crystal brook that glistens
Running clear, it beckons yonder
A mother's love so precious
It's heaven sent with wonder.

To live life without love's glory
Reflects tide without the moon
A world desolate of love
Would breed the darkest gloom
Love creates such happiness
The life blood of our soul
It's a mystery of colour
Love's a beautiful rainbow.

Maxine Godfrey

WISHING

Should I be granted just one wish,
A wish nurtured in my heart,
T'would be to spend our lives together
And never, ever part

Hand in hand we would stroll together
Down the pathway of true love,
To share a kiss, a warm embrace,
'Neath the moon and stars above.

Within your strong protective arms
Nought shall I ever fear,
You are my steady rock on which to lean
When troubled times appear.

Your charming smile and witty humour
Brighten the darkest days,
My life you fill with love and joy
In so many different ways.

Always remain beside me,
My lover and best friend
To share our joys and sorrows
Until life's journey ends.

Barbara Sowden

EXPO

Feelings visibly expressed,
Vigorously unrepressed,
Like a kiss upon the cheek,
Supersede what people speak,
Show a bond between the pair
Viewers couldn't know or share.
But, a kiss has many strings:
Catalysing roots and wings,
Healing hearts and soothing pains,
Causing youth to fill the veins.
So, the body, soul and mind
Demonstrate to humankind;
Lots of kisses, love and hugs
Are the strongest wonder drugs.

Geoff Storer

I LOVE YOU

'I love you' he whispered gently in my ear,
Words uttered on false lips - a serpents tongue -
And there the deceit had just begun;
And yet I chose to believe - I wanted to.
The need for affirmation - nothing new.
Spent my life chasing rainbows, wishing on stars,
Trod many roads, played many parts.
Always on the outside looking in;
Wondering why I never fit in?
Wondering which way the wind will blow me next?
The search for love my eternal quest.
I've walked the silver lining of every cloud
And basked in the glory of an applauding crowd.
I've let the sun caress me - the sea protect me.
I've drowned in love - danced with death
And hurt the people who've loved me best.
Yet the love for which I have true need
Comes from within - called self-belief;
And until I can turn and look inside,
To face my truths and face my lies,
To exercise the hurt and pain,
My quest will always be in vain;
Because you can run - but never hide;
When the only path left is the one inside;
It's time to take courage - face my fears -
Liberate myself of yesteryears;
To face my reflection, without wanting to hide,
To stop feeling guilt and start feeling pride;
To say to myself and know that it's true,
These three small words - 'I love you!'

Emma Clifton

PARTING

Sweet lips, soft lips, cool lips,
Run my finger over your sleeping lips
Gently, smoothly, so secure
That your kisses are for me.
Strong kisses, burning kisses,
Want you now kisses,
Roll around the floor kisses
Too much wasted time
No time to waste.
Thinking of you all week
For the passions of a weekend.
You whimper, your breath through lips and teeth
Echoes your dream of romance
A strong woman in control
Equals in our love
Defeating the cancers that gnawed into our emptinesses
But you know much more than me
Know your future and mine
Know that our futures are not divine
That these moments are ours, the perfection we desire
Know that right now is not our tomorrows
Our parting is not sweet sorrows.

David Pennington

ACTION MAN

Beer goggles firmly in place,
I sway toward you, and smile at your face,
Legs swinging and head swaying too,
I put on my charm face, grin lamely at you.

Head tilted, I swoon for the kill,
Legs stutter, feel slightly ill.
Lips sliding and tongue feeling too
What am I doing, stood here with you?

Stumble outside into a bush,
Pull you close, enjoy the rush
Play the game, who's better, who's best?
Hands draw an outline, on your small white vest.

Tussle my hair, exhale on you there,
While Monets on high stools, whisper and stare.
Lucid a moment, I take in your face,
Break realisation, with hasty embrace.

Out comes your cousin,
To ruin our fun,
Clutches your hand,
And away you run.

Inside I swagger,
To face all the noise.
Cheers from the masses,
Hoots from bad boys.

You take what is not yours
And get what you can.
My new persona
Is called 'Action Man'.

Luke Williams

ACTION REPLAY

Your beautiful face renders me gibberish in your wake,
I do not function in your presence,
My eyes rove over you, head to toe,
My fingers, they itch to touch you,
You took a kiss,
I was inspired,
I felt your pain, your need, your must,
I wanted you to show me your trust,
A while past, many days,
We kissed again, the effect much as the same,
I eased your need to show my love,
To care was all I'm guilty of,
To be rejected is hard to bare,
But through the doubts and aching despair,
My head in hands rewinds and plays the stolen kiss with fingers running
Through our hair,
A million and one actions I replay your beautiful face . . .

D P R

BREAKFAST IN BED

2 cups clink,
In an echoey kitchen -
Down a dusty, wooden, sunlit hallway

I Breath . . .

The glorious smell
Of percolating coffee
Drifts into the bedroom and over last nights clothes

I half-turn . . .

Some long remembered
Olden day tune
Is being gently whistled through slightly crooked teeth

I stretch . . . slowly.

Padded footsteps;
Warmed croissants;
A soft peck on my left cheek which makes me cry.

Emma Gordon